Family Fare

Family Fare

Thoughts on Family Living

by
Paul Martin

Beacon Hill Press of Kansas City
Kansas City, Missouri

Contents

Foreword

Paul Martin likes people . . . all kinds . . . all ages . . . everywhere. For 30 years he has traveled over the world, holding revivals and crusades ("Spiritual Improvement Weeks," he calls them). If you ever hear Paul Martin speak, you'll get the feeling that he really cares about your hurts and needs. Whether he is speaking or writing, God's love seems to shine through this "servant of Jesus"!

Paul Martin is a devoted husband and father, so he speaks from practical experience as well as biblical knowledge.

This book is divided into short, intriguing chapters which only take a few moments to read. Some chapters are humorous as well as serious—for example, "Little Old Ladies in Tennis Shoes"—while others bring fresh thoughts on needed subjects—for example, "Move Out."

Since he admits in his preface that his wife, Monica, has worked with him in producing this interesting "family album," the reader can be assured of a "feminine touch," which should make reading this volume by a well-known, popular speaker and author even more interesting and spiritually rewarding.

—DONALD J. GIBSON
Executive Secretary, Department of Evangelism
Church of the Nazarene

Preface

To: The Reader
From: The Author
Subject: How to Use *Family Fare*

This book is simple and in alphabetical order. It wasn't intended for study, but mostly for inspiration or direction. The table of contents enables you to find what strikes you, for the day, in a few seconds. The messages are short. You can "dip in" any place you like and lay it aside just as quickly. I saw this sort of arrangement in a business organization book and liked it.

It would be foolish for me to try to counsel, psychoanalyze, or go deeply into the subject of family relations, adjustments, marital stress—and bliss. So there is little of that here. Yet I've lived awhile, learned of the Lord, loved my family and my home, and struggled to be a growing Christian. And along the way, opinions, ideas, and hints to better living have taken form. So I have set them down . . . they are here . . . for better or for worse.

Two principles guided the preparation:

1. *God is loving, good, real, available, and open.* Through Jesus we see His love for us. Yes, "God commendeth his love toward us, in that, while we were yet sinners, Christ died for us" (Rom. 5:8).

2. *The very nature of love means the Lover longs for the growth, improvement, and personal well-being of the loved one.* God's answers are best. God's way is the right way. As Ezra stopped at the river of Ahava to find the right way for himself and

his little ones, so may we . . . at a crossroads, at closed doors, at any time . . . search for God's way.

Much of what I see makes me laugh. (Laughing is better than fussing.) Crying is a part of living too! Also, we laugh and cry at different things. You may cry at what I hoped would make you smile.

Monica, my wife, has worked with me on this book. Her wisdom, extensive reading, and loving understanding come through often.

So read it, forget what you can, remember what you should. And the Lord bless you.

—PAUL MARTIN

*In the house of the righteous is much
treasure.*

PROV. 15:6

Around the House

How is it around your house? Around the house
is where you live. Around the house others may
live. How is it there? Hectic, happy, comfortable,
carefree, cantankerous . . . around the house? It is
what you make it. One house stands, one falls. One
can stand the storm, one cannot. There is so much
that is precious around the house. You are there . . .
so tell me . . . how is it in your home?

There is no magic, automatic, electronic producer
of love around the house. We are not computers.
We are sons, daughters, brothers, sisters, husbands,
wives, grandparents around the house. It is a peo-
ple-house. The chairs, the beds, the tables, the gadgets are for people. So we really live like we want
. . . around the house.

Take a look around the house. Anything missing?
Window out? Fix it. Faucet dripping? Quiet it. Floor
dirty? Sweep it. Foundation sagging? Restore it. An-
ger flaring? Check it. Jealousy rising? Settle it. Suspicion lingering? Talk about it. We fix the

11

gadgetlike stuff so quickly . . . what about people problems, cares, and trials? Do they go unattended?

There is help around the house—if God is there. Not in the furniture nor the carport. He is in the thoughts, the will, the affection of the people . . . the family. He is the Friend of the family. He it is who makes it right around the house! He comes by invitation. He stays as we care for Him, trust Him, obey Him, and love Him.

It is great to have God around the house, in the house, the strength of the house, the Lord of the house. Be sure He is in your heart and in your house. Put Him first, seek Him regularly, obey Him carefully. There will be joy, peace, and love . . . and these are treasures . . . "in the house of the righteous."

A man hath joy by the answer of his mouth: and a word spoken in due season, how good is it!

—PROV. 15:23

All Through the House

"Not a creature was stirring, not even a mouse." . . . The charm of that great Christmas poem, "'Twas the night before Christmas" . . . what a feeling of anticipation it expresses! The whole house seems on tiptoe for a glorious surprise.

All right, let's say a good thing or two for anticipation, suspense, expectation. They do so much for family fun and frolic.

It may be that anticipation is greater than realization. That planning is as big as doing. Anyway, together it means a real good time will be had by all.

Anticipation means planning ahead as far as possible. The longer we look ahead, the longer the fun of planning. Get some good times lined up for the summer, for the school holiday, down the line. Plan ahead.

Anticipation works well when we plan together. Happy hours spent in getting ready: the camping area found; fishing gear repaired, restocked, and even tried out on the lawn; responsibility designated; lists made of things to do, things to take, things to leave home, things to get the neighbors to do. Some studying up on the project helps. For a month or two . . . one hour a week, or a part of one day a week could be set aside as *Countdown*, (27 days to Yellowstone or camp meeting or Disneyland —or all three).

Anticipation means carrying through happily. Not a threat to keep the family in shape. Planning, interaction means difference of opinion—surely! Yet, this is no time for stubbornness. It is a happy time. Be generous, thoughtful; take time to listen; and share the decision making. The big day will be a better day if you let them help plan it . . . freely . . . happily.

There are a hundred good days before the trip, the graduation, the wedding, the big ball game, the youth camp, the overseas jaunt . . . so make the most of every day of preparation. Why not!

In the fear of the Lord is strong confidence: and his children shall have a place of refuge.

—PROV. 14:26

All in the Family

"It takes two to make a marriage, and it takes two to break it." I heard that on a soap opera one afternoon. Then there was another program that said some things to people . . . "All in the Family." It dared to bring into the open some secret fears, prejudices, follies, and hopes of a family. I didn't like everything on the program, but at least it made us think.

Have you ever thought of this: Everything you need for a wholesome, happy, loving family is here. It's all in the family. 'Tis a pity to dream of some great lucky change that will come. 'Tis a pity to stake our hopes on a better house, more gadgets, and a rich uncle! The ingredients for a good home are here . . . in your family . . . in mine.

People are here. They are the family. People capable of understanding, patience, forgiveness, and love.

Keep this idea first for a while: that we can make the changes in our home . . . we can talk it out . . . we can face the facts. We can live in love. What I'm trying to say is that no one can force misery, suspicion, bitterness, carelessness on your home. What is there is all in the family!

As I say that, I know that God is there. You know . . . God is here, there, ready, available, anxious . . . and so able to draw us together, heal our hurts, lift our sagging hopes, and warm our hearts with love.

Listen, the next time you are all together, maybe around the dinner table . . . take a good look . . . it's all in the family . . . the privilege of a forgiving spirit, the pleasure of sharing, the joys of thoughtfulness, the peace that Jesus gives. It is there . . . the key to good living . . . use it.

Nor of men sought we glory, neither of you, nor yet of others, when we might have been burdensome.

—1 THESS. 2:6

Big Loads

Here's a load that is almost impossible to carry (they just don't make luggage large enough)—the load of making a living. But we have to do it. It is one of the obligations of life. It seems to be a law of existence: If we eat, we must work—must do it gladly. The blessings of the home, the joys of the family are ample reward for the labor.

Yet every now and then I meet a man who is never satisfied. He is carrying a far bigger load. The drive to make lots of money, the comfort, the peace he seeks for his family by making life easy is lost in the worry, the separation, and sometimes the cheap means he uses.

Jesus talked about a man who had lots of money but lost it all when he died. In his torment the rich man expressed three things: (1) God gave me many good things . . . I didn't share them; (2) I had five brothers, but I cannot help them; (3) I waited too late to pray. (These may be my words as much as the rich man's, but this is what the parable says to me.)

16

About all he had perished with him. It was a big load.

The load of making a living isn't all that bad, is it? Let's do it with joy and spend with love.

Keep thy heart with all diligence; for
out of it are the issues of life.

—Prov. 4:23

Concealed Weapons

It Is a Federal Crime to
  Carry Concealed Weapons.
    Passengers and Baggage
      Subject to Search.

That's the way the notice reads in the air terminal.

Does your family really believe you? A family can take a lot of heartache, disappointment, and even disaster . . . if they trust each other . . . no concealed weapons!

Here are some weapons that always destroy:

Concealed sins, secret misconduct

  Unforgiving spirit, deep bitterness . . . lingering, gnawing

    Fear, unwilling to trust, in no position to trust

Let love do the searching. Love forgives and forgets. A clean heart and an honest confession bring peace. It is a good beginning . . . again.

Let love heal the hurt, bathe and soothe the

wound, bring confidence to the sinned-against and the sinning.

Let love ease the fears. An honest heart has nothing to fear but fear itself.

Let's walk in the garden of trust . . . play in the garden of peace . . . work in the garden of openness.

OK! Have a good day.

I know that, whatsoever God doeth, it shall be for ever: nothing can be put to it, nor any thing taken from it.

—ECCLES. 3:14

What Dies with You?

Truth? No.

Your tears? Yes.

Your pain, your frustration? Yes.

Your good works? They need not. The life song you wrote may be sung in other lives.

Your love? No. It will be purer, better here where you loved . . . and there where love is.

Your sins? Yes. The fact is that they are already in "the sea of God's forgetfulness." They will be remembered against you no more. The God of forgiveness did a thorough work when you repented.

Your sins? In another sense, no. If forgiveness is neglected, suffering continues . . . and some suffering continues because, before being forgiven, we have hurt others and cannot now stop sin's senseless power.

Your car? Oh, yes, it died several times while you were alive. Other things you think so necessary go when you go . . . TV, fine clothes, diamonds, poodle dogs, guns, stereos, snowmobiles, and fishing gear . . . You can't take them with you.

Those you led to Christ? . . . No . . . not really, for you shall meet again. Christ promised that. So let us give a little more attention to that which will not perish . . . in a perishing world. It is good family exercise.

◈◈◈◈◈

To every thing there is a season, and a time to every purpose under the heaven.

—ECCLES. 3:1

Don't Rush It

A blue-eyed blond, three years of age, stood in front of me and, hands on hips, gave me this jingle:

Two blue eyes and a little cute figure—
Stand back, boys, till I get a little bigger.

But how we rush things. We seem to want the children to be adults. We have a deathly fear our little girl might miss marriage. We are a pain-in-the-neck to the umpire at the Little League games. We just can't let the kids play.

You know all these things. But the point of the lesson is—let life move at its own pace. Girls can be tomboys if they want for a while. Boys can play with teddy bears if they want, too. Daughter might

21

not care till she's 30, and George might care before he's 14.

Then there comes the time when we try to reverse the whole business. We iron our wrinkles, dip our hair, dress like a teen-ager (or try to), and talk like one. What a pity! No one really likes it.

This then is a call to quit pushing either way. Enjoy the days as they come. Be yourself and let the good times come and let them go. There are better things, in other ways, that are coming, and every time has its reason and joy.

∞⊙♨⊙∞

Keep thy tongue from evil, and thy lips from speaking guile.

—Ps. 34:13

Dog Bites Man

"Dog Bites Man" . . . common headline.

"Man Bites Dog" . . . not very common.

"Man Bites Man" . . . almost every day in one way or another.

Some good friend told me the story of a man who was bit by a dog. When the health officer tested the dog, he found it was rabid. Immediately upon hearing this report, the victim began to write on a pad furiously.

"We can give you serum, sir," said the health of-

22

ficer; "you don't need to write your last will and testament."

"I'm not writing my will," cried the bitten brother, "I'm writing a list of 10 people I want to bite!"

All right, turn this around and make a list today of 10 people you want to help, encourage, lift, and serve, as if you were afflicted by the infectious disease of love.

Start with your family. They are the closest: your husband, your wife, the children, the in-laws.

Go to your pastor and church friends.

Then your neighbors, those with whom you work. Spread the good words of appreciation and love.

I wrote, "As if you were afflicted . . ." This is what happens when we make Jesus Lord of our lives. We are "bitten" by Him; He is in us; we are in Him. We spread His love by personal contact with others. They become "afflicted" . . . and it grows and grows and grows.

If you have been afflicted by His spirit, then make your list and start today.

Who hath put wisdom in the inward parts? Or who hath given understanding to the heart?

—JOB 38:36

A Week Expert

Since much of my life has been spent in one-week evangelistic campaigns, 30 to 40 times a year, I tend to cut life down into one week. I can be so knowledgeable, so smart in one week. Not quite an instant authority, but almost. What a pity.

The El Toro Cafe was advertised as serving authentic Mexican food. Though new, its decor and arrangements were made to look old. The food was prepared by a Chinese cook whom they sent to Mexico for one week to learn the Spanish flavor. He became an expert in a week.

Now is the time to tell you that there is no substitute for careful preparation, wise experience, and discipline.

For instance: One doesn't become a man or woman of prayer instantly. No, we learn to pray by praying.

A good father, an understanding father doesn't just come to life as the baby does. The art of under-

24

standing, the art of love and patience takes a lot of practice.

Happy homes don't just happen. All in the home, trying together, can make a happy home. Good things, like honesty, sharing, caring, loving are the products of discipline and patience. It takes more than a week to make them a wholesome habit.

Well, Master, thou hast said the truth: for there is one God; and there is none other but he.

—MARK 12:32

Failing Gods

Sir, I was startled at this headline: "U.S. Gods Are Failing." And you know it is true. The article went on to say that America's two gods—Wall Street and the auto industry—were falling. I trust this recession will not last (1975), but the whole world is groaning right now, and gods have failed. People are fearful, apprehensive, and depressed.

The gods of gold, silver, and brass always fail. Gadget gods, cheaper than gold, fall too. Paper gods, like influence, position, peer patronizing, pass too.

The real God never fails, and really there are no other gods. It is simply that we seek amiss. Our mistake, our failure is in our foolish search. For God, as Jesus shows us, is so approachable, so dependable.

Brother, let me ask five personal questions:

1. Do you really believe that the knowledge of God, a personal experience with God, is worth more than things . . . gaudy things . . . plain things . . . even good things?

2. Do you seek God's presence, His will, His love as earnestly as you seek other gods?

3. Do your closest friends really believe you are God's?

4. Were you to meet God tonight, would life be completely lost—out of balance?

5. It is time to look carefully at yourself . . . isn't it? And make this a spiritual improvement time.

⊷❦⊶

And all that sat in the council, looking stedfastly on him, saw his face as it had been the face of an angel.
—ACTS 6:15

A Good Face

A good face in a good place is worth seeing.

It is not always so, but life is often written on the face . . . a clear eye, a kind expression, a happy face.

So I got to thinking about good faces in good places.

In the terrible tornado of Xenia, Ohio, there was the calm, determined face of Pastor Rickey among 150 frightened schoolchildren. The building wrecked, and not a child hurt. A strong face in a wrecked place.

With the smell of tear gas very evident, yelling, angry young people all around, there was a compassionate, prayerful face. It was a Campus Crusade staffer, anxious to tell of the Christ of peace. He led the student body president to the Lord. A peaceful face in a disturbed place.

It was a half-burned house; the father had died as he saved his child. Soon a caring face was at the door. It was a doctor's wife. She stayed two weeks, right with the lonely family. A caring face in a burned-out place. Miracles were these.

I saw a tearful, comforting face on the missionary as she listened patiently to the bereaved husband. Perhaps it is a common scene, but a precious one. A sharing face in a desperate place.

In a family circle, heads bowed. The Bible read. There was a loving, quiet face asking for the peace of God. A prayerful face in a common place.

How about your home, your work, your hard times, good times? How about your face? Is it peaceful, strong, determined, loving? Let the Face-changer, the Lord, come to you in your place.

Thou shalt take no gift: for the gift blindeth the wise, and perverteth the words of the righteous.

—EXOD. 23:8

The Golden Rule

What is the golden rule? Is it "He who has the gold makes the rules"?

There is a lot of truth in that statement . . . yes, too much truth. People with money turn our heads, affect our decisions, gain our love, while the poor seem strangely wrong. But the poor are not necessarily wrong. I think it was Abe Lincoln who said, "God must love the poor, He made so many of them."

Of course, there is respect due those whose judgment and discipline have helped them prosper. But those who do not prosper are worthy too. Men may make money, but money never makes men . . . it actually ruins many.

Here are a few simple questions to ask yourself . . . quietly.

1. Do I really wink at the excesses of the prosperous and gripe at the problems of the poor?

2. Do I show those close to me that dollars are not my God?

3. Am I fair with God with my tithe and offerings? (If 10 percent tithing bothers, try 20 percent for a while, and you will stop bothering.)

4. Just what do those who love me think about my attitude toward money?

5. Oh, the perils of being overextended . . . how do I feel about it?

You know, money and love are alike . . . in one way at least. Khalil Gibran said, "Money is like love: It kills slowly and painfully the one who withholds it, and it enlivens the other who turns it upon his fellowman."

Giving, then, is the key, the golden key. Listen to this—you will like it—"He gives not best who gives most, but he gives most who gives best."

So if you cannot give largely, give freely.

Marriage is honourable in all, and the bed undefiled: but whoremongers and adulterers God will judge.

—HEB. 13:4

A Good Marriage

Rev. Charles Higgins, pastor of First Church of the Nazarene at Nampa, Ida., preaches annually a series of sermons on the family, marriage, home, and children. I listened to several of these sermons.

They are good, helpful, and Christ-centered. I borrowed these thoughts from him.

Principles of a Good Marriage

1. A good marriage is not necessarily a perfect marriage.

2. Give the husband-and-wife relationship first place. God first, mate second, children third. Many marriages have little left after the children are gone. Parenthood is temporary, marriage is permanent.

3. We must keep alive the attitude of courtships. Make it easy to love each other. Another dimension of this is sexual fulfillment.

4. Be quick to forgive, and forgive before it is asked. Never remind the other of the past.

5. Assume your husband or wife is your best friend. Develop the security of feeling safe with one another.

6. Cultivate a sense of humor. Laughing together is a good tonic.

7. A husband and wife should develop a spiritual relationship with each other. Praying together does help us to stay together.

Read these again . . . they are helpful. And thank you, Charles Higgins.

*My lovers and my friends stand aloof
from my sore, and my kinsmen stand
afar off.*

—Ps. 38:11

Hangers-on

It was unforgettable. Here we were, an evangelistic team from the United States, in Rio de Janeiro. The teen-age son of a missionary was escorting us to our evening service about 16 miles out of the city. Mainly for the experience, he took us on the Rio commuter at the rush hour. I have never been in or on such a crowded train. We were squeezed, pulled, pushed on and off. My friend, Paul Skiles, claimed his feet didn't touch the train floor at any time. Dr. Uerkvitz, our musician, lost every button on his coat. And in order to get off at our station, we had to smash our way, like a goal-line drive in football.

It is the *pingente* that worry the police and the train company. The word means "hangers-on." Dangling precariously from doors and windows, crouching on the roofs suicidally close to the electric wires, they swarm into the city center daily. They do it for several reasons: Some jump on at the last minute to save having to pay fare; some do it for thrills; some, to show off. Many spend the whole day swinging from train to train.

Dangerous? Yes, every week some are killed and many more hurt.

Here's the point I want to make. Life is complicated enough, and our homes are overloaded with problems, so don't be a hanger-on. Make the effort to get in where the pressure is . . . of course there is pressure living together, around the house. And it takes a lot of caring and sharing and patience and faithfulness to make a house a home. Don't just look on, show off, run out, escape the "fare" of living. You are needed. Your judgment, your strength, just *you* . . . all are valuable to your home. So get right in and live and love.

⚜

In the mouth of the foolish is a rod of pride: but the lips of the wise shall preserve them.
—PROV. 14:3

How Do I Know?

"How do you know, Mr. Martin?" Do you hear this question often? I do. How do we know the best answer . . . the right way?

Before I give an answer, let me say this. Many times and in many situations, to make an honest decision, even if you change it later, is better than indecision. Delay and postponement are often harmful. A thoughtful, honest decision brings peace.

When deciding, remember . . . God gave you judgment—use it. Most of the time, the right way is what you think is right! Do it until you think better.

Praying is important. Praying clears the atmosphere . . . helps arrange priorities . . . brings motives into focus! And God hears prayer.

Some answers are found immediately in the Bible. "Whatsoever things are true, whatsoever things are honest, whatsoever things are just, whatsoever things are pure, whatsoever things are lovely, whatsoever things are of good report . . . think on these things" (Phil. 4:8).

Some things can be talked over . . . by a family or with a good friend.

And how about this—I found a quote that says some of this far better than I. George MacDonald, British teacher, says, "How am I to know a thing is true? By doing what you know to be true, and calling nothing true until you see it to be true; by shutting your mouth until the truth opens it." Such good advice!

When he saw the wind boisterous, he was afraid; and beginning to sink, he cried, saying, Lord, save me.
　　　　　　　　　—MATT. 14:30

Help

Calling for help isn't cowardly . . . it's sensible, that's for sure.

Calling for help . . . may mean you were not too lazy to try something new!

Calling for help . . . Self-sufficiency doesn't really help, does it?

Calling for help . . . Jesus is close.

Calling for help . . . We are helpless in ourselves; it is so good you found that out.

Calling for help . . . Others are sinking too; they may hear your cry and get courage to call.

Calling for help . . . I do often.

In every thing give thanks: for this is the will of God in Christ Jesus concerning you.

—1 THESS. 5:18

In Everything Give Thanks

The key word in this Bible verse is "in." Not after it is all over, not when I have had time to see it clearly, not before it happens . . . but while I am *in it* . . . in the heat of the problem, in the midst of the struggle, while it is on, I will give thanks. (What a long, complicated sentence!) It simply means, let us learn to give thanks in the midst of it all, good or bad, easy or hard.

If Jesus is really Lord of our lives, then what comes to us, God allows. The Bible tells us God allowed Jesus to suffer, and He is sensitive to our needs (Heb. 4:13-14). We can thank Him.

As we trust the Lord, our Lord, we know He promised to work everything for good to those who love Him (Rom. 8:28). We then can thank Him "in all things," for we know God will work something good for us.

I'm not sure I have grown to this place, but I'm trying—right in the dark place, before it gets light, on the steep grade, with lots of questions. I am trying to "thank God" for letting it come, for He has a good thing for me in it. Now don't toss this thought out before you try it.

As we thank Him, let us share with others, not boastfully, but happily, that through it all, we are trusting Jesus. Through it all, praise the Lord!

*Unto man he said, Behold, the fear of
the Lord, that is wisdom.*

—Job 28:28

Just Suppose

Let's have a little word fun. Supposing. Gives me
a chance to do some meddling and having fun as
well.

Just suppose the Lord would begin tomorrow to
make people as sick as they claim to be on Sunday.

Just suppose the Lord should make people as poor
as they claim to be when asked to give to the church.

Just suppose the Lord should have everyone
stoned to death for covetousness as was Achan.

Just suppose your family told the real reason you
missed work.

Just suppose they believed you when you said
you didn't really care.

Just suppose Jesus came back for one week to
your town, your street; would you be comfortable?

Just suppose you could look down the road and
see what the results will be of some actions today.

Just suppose you prayed as much as you say you
do.

Just suppose you had 10 hours to live.

Just suppose you were the only one left to make the big decision.

Just suppose it all turned out as you were afraid it would . . . and suppose it didn't.

Supposing is fun at times. But changing life is God's business. With His help, we can live and serve as if eternity is close. And it is.

⋘◉⫸

Hew thee two tables of stone like unto the first: and I will write upon these tables the words that were in the first tables, which thou brakest.

—EXOD. 34:1

Just Try Again

If just you and I were talking together, and you told me of a tough problem you were facing . . . I would say, "Try again."

If you told me that you had tried a hundred times to win someone to Christ . . . I would say, "Try again."

If you told me you were struggling with some distasteful habit . . . I would say, "Try again."

If you said, "I've worked with them, again and again. They don't seem to be any closer to Jesus than when I first met them. I've had such a burden for this young couple. But I'm going to quit trying" . . . I would say, "Try again."

If you told me that you were struggling to forget a bitter experience, wanting really to bury it . . . but there it is haunting . . . I would say, "Try again."

Like picking up a crossword puzzle you have set aside . . . like backing off and looking at the problem . . . like asking a friend one more time for his suggestions . . . just trying again is worth the try.

Before you give up . . . ask yourself these questions:

"Did I pray about it?"

"Did I really try everything that I could to see this thing settled?"

"Did I sleep on it awhile and work with a rested mind?"

"Did I consult someone for suggestions and try them?"

"Did I take this tough emotional problem . . . as one of the problems of living . . . and work carefully, prayerfully with it?"

A good Christian lady said this during testimony time in a meeting recently: "Living is a struggle, but I would rather struggle to heaven than skip to hell." Amen, and again, Amen.

Every tongue should confess that Jesus Christ is Lord, to the glory of God the Father.

—Phil. 2:11

King of Kings

Since I am no singer, it is amazing how often a song gets stuck in my mind and heart. I hear it over and over again. Today it is: "King of my life I crown Thee now; Thine shall the glory be."

To me this is the heart of the Spirit-filled life, the sanctified life . . . making Jesus Lord of all. Not just saying it, or singing it, but a fact of life . . . your life, my life, through and through.

This experience has three parts. The first is believing that God's way is the right way for you. It is an unchangeable, almost stubborn commitment to the way of the Lord.

Second, if I truly believe His will is best, then I let Him have full control. I yield whatever talent, plans, friends, and my very self to the Lord to be totally His. (Rom. 12:1-2 says it well, "I beseech you therefore, brethren, by the mercies of God, that ye present your bodies a living sacrifice, holy, acceptable unto God, which is your reasonable service. And be not conformed to this world: but be ye transformed by the renewing of your mind, that ye may prove what is that good, and acceptable, and perfect, will of God.")

Third, now I can receive the Spirit. "That we might receive the promise of the Spirit through faith" (Gal. 3:14). It is not an emotion, it is the deep conviction that God has done what He promises to do. He is Lord, King of my life.

Now I can *live* in the Spirit.

What man is there of you, whom if his son ask bread, will give him a stone? Or if he ask a fish, will he give him a serpent?

—MATT. 7:9-10

For Crying Out Loud

"What do you want . . . for crying out loud!" Used to be a slang phrase. (Really should be "loudly," too, they tell me.) Crying means someone wants something . . . he is afraid, he's hurt, he is crying to express it. Jesus said, "When he asks for bread would you give him a stone? When he asks for a fish, do you give a serpent?" Have we asked why people cry . . . the real young, the real old . . . in between? Maybe if they talked . . . they would say, "I want love . . . love that takes time to listen. Love that understands . . . or tries. Love that remembers."

"I want direction. I'm afraid of myself, of the things I feel and see. I am learning I cannot go back. Guide me . . . show me the disciplined way, the good way.

"I want God. It's empty inside. I was made to hope, to believe, to worship. I want to pray with you . . . believe with you . . . worship with you."

You may not have little ones around, but big people, neighbors . . . crying out loud. Will you give

43

them more than a stony stare? Give them more than an irritable, self-centered serpent!

Crying gets on the nerves . . . let it get on your heart too.

❧❀❧

I have been young, and now am old; yet have I not seen the righteous forsaken, nor his seed begging bread.
—Ps. 37:25

Little Old Ladies in Tennis Shoes

I don't know where the phrase "Little old ladies in tennis shoes" originated. It sounds like something Herb Caen of the *San Francisco Chronicle* would invent. The prototype is often seen as a belligerent conservative, slightly paranoid, tending to be a busybody. The little old lady in tennis shoes is also a spunky, sweet, old girl, hard as hickory and a lovable rebel.

I've known a good many little old ladies. Hardly any wore tennis shoes. And I love them. They are good company.

I thought of these things too: Little old ladies were young and pretty not long ago, and they are beautiful today. Pay attention.

Little old ladies have loved, have been loved, and want to share love now. Take time to cherish.

Little old ladies have memories. Memories are yesterday's high and low moments carried along. They may be mixed and colored some, but listen. Enjoy them too . . . reliving them is often better than experiencing them the first time.

Little old ladies are frail. Be gentle. There are enough others in the world on whom to practice toughness. God is getting them ready for much better things.

Little old ladies are unsteady. They need a strong hand, a big heart. How are yours?

Little old ladies are special to God, "even down to white heads." So there just must be an extra blessing for those who care for God's special ones, the world's perky ones, "little old ladies."

Blessed are the meek: for they shall inherit the earth.

—Matt. 5:5

Meet Mr. and Mrs. Meek

The Meeks are mentioned by the Lord in the great sermon . . . "Blessed are the meek: for they shall inherit the earth." Who are the meek? Dr. John A. Knight says that the meek are those who accept themselves just as they are . . . no struggling to build ego . . . no feeling of inadequacy . . . just as they are . . . humbly confident.

Mr. and Mrs. Meek quarrel very little! They seem to have a profound respect for each other. For they not only accept themselves as they are . . . but accept each other. They are not angels and they know it. But they are not fiends either . . . and they know that too. There is harmony and peace in respect . . . in real sharing!

Mr. and Mrs. Meek are refreshingly honest . . . and helpful. In a crisscross age, plastic and unreal, wholesome honesty is very attractive. Neighbors like to come over . . . and be real! No "put on," no "putting anyone down." Yes, it is always good to go to the Meeks'.

Mr. and Mrs. Meek are trusting in Christ! They know how much they need Him. Once they trusted in themselves . . . now in Jesus. Once they sadly knew the bitter taste of sin and selfishness. Now there is peace in Christ.

❧✾❧

None of these things move me . . . so
that I might finish my course with joy.
— ACTS 20:24

Move Out

I saw an ad in a Los Angeles newspaper, full page, which read, "After the kids move out, maybe you should too," and that's what we do.

Move out of the busy, feeling-needed routine to a dull, boring, meaningless life.

Some move to a reckless, shallow, hectic life. The restraints they had for the family are thrown aside. This too is unproductive . . . often becomes miserable. This is sad. We move away from each other to lonely, selfish ways. The joy of being together, ah— the privilege is lost somehow. This is a really bad move.

Others move into bickering, blaming, arguing ways. There may have never been "oneness" at home, and now it really shows.

It seems fairly easy too to move away from God. After all, we don't have to pray for the kids' sakes now nor even go to church with them. We can do what we've always wanted to do.

If it is moving time, let me suggest some better moves.

Let's move even nearer to God. He is real, so dependable, so true. Talk about Him even more, talk to Him, together, more often.

Let's move closer to each other. Find new areas of oneness, better ways to work together. Now we need each other more than ever. We can share our work plans, business problems, homework, fun times.

Let's move into some new fields of self-improvement. After all, you've spent much of your life together raising the family, sending them to school, solving their problems, settling their fights . . . now it is time to restart for yourself. Perhaps it is back-to-school time, or travel time, or volunteer service time. I don't know, but it is *your* time. Use it well.

Look at it this way: You and yours are people too . . . loving, caring, important people in the family of God. As the house gets empty, fill it with more love, more prayer, more fun, more things to do. You really don't have to move anywhere; just fill what you have with His glory.

⋖◉⋅⋗

There are also many other things which Jesus did.

—JOHN 21:25

Many Ways

"There are so many ways." This phrase came rushing to mind recently. It is a good thought; it inspired me.

It is one of the tools of the evil one to say, "There is no way. It is hopeless. No way." Remember, good friend, the enemy cannot tell the truth. He is a continual liar. Don't listen.

There is no real limit to what God can do. There were even scores of things that John remembered about Jesus that were not written. So many, he said, that the whole world could hardly contain the books that could be written (John 21:25).

So here are some things to say to yourself, often.

There are many ways to face our failures that are better than running away. The fears will pass if we squarely, honestly admit our failure and begin again.

There are many ways to meet our problems other than blaming someone. There is no peace in the heart of the blamer.

There are many ways to show our love other than just the same way all the time. Love is an art. It can be learned, encouraged, deepened. Search for fresh ways.

There are many ways to learn more about God. His ways are exciting ways. His Word is full of new things. Let's find these other ways and try them.

His father had not displeased him at any time in saying, Why hast thou done so?

—1 KINGS 1:6

No-nos

Let's make a list of things, irritable things—perhaps foolish things—that can be left out of our homelife. After you have read these, make another list of your own.

Don't con anybody. (*Con* comes from the term *confidenceman*, one who tricks, deceives, flatters to get his own way.) Not your wife, not your husband, not your children, not your brothers and sisters, not your neighbors . . . and don't con yourself either.

Don't always do it all yourself. They may not do it as well, or as quickly as you, but it is still better for all if they do it.

Don't all the time pull your rank (a phrase that means using your title or position to force your way or opinion). An army colonel I know, called "Big Red," is a favorite with the regulars because he insists that the officers, himself included, do the running, push-ups, and training, just as the others.

Don't overkill. (This word means excessive, too much.) Overdressed, oversensitive, overcritical, overorganized, even overplanned. Just too much . . . not enough left for spontaneity, for happiness.

Don't remember everything. You are not an elephant. A good forgetter brings peace of mind, heals old wounds, lifts weary hearts, and keeps you at rest as well.

Now write your no-nos.

⋘◉⋙

Though our outward man perish, yet the inward man is renewed day by day.

—2 Cor. 4:16

Not Growing Old

They say that I am growing old,
I've heard them tell it times untold,
In language plain and bold—
But I'm not growing old.
This frail old shell in which I dwell
Is growing old, I know full well—
But I am not the shell.

What if my hair is turning grey?
Grey hairs are honorable, they say.
What if my eyesight's growing dim?
I still can see to follow Him
Who sacrificed His life for me
Upon the cross of Calvary.

What should I care if time's old plough
Has left its furrows on my brow?

51

Another house, not made with hand,
Awaits me in the glory land.

What though I falter in my walk?
What though my tongue refuse to talk?
I still can tread the narrow way,
I still can watch, and praise and pray.

My hearing may not be as keen
As in the past it may have been,
Still I can hear my Saviour say
In whispers soft, "This is the way."

The outward man, do what I can
To lengthen out this life's short span,
Shall perish, and return to dust,
As everything in nature must.
The inward man, the Scriptures say,
Is growing stronger every day.

Then how can I be growing old
When safe within my Saviour's fold?
Ere long my soul shall fly away,
And leave this tenement of clay,
This robe of flesh I'll drop and rise
To seize the "everlasting prize."
I'll meet you on the streets of gold,
And prove that I'm not growing old.

—JOHN E. ROBERTS

That they all may be one; as thou, Father, art in me, and I in thee, that they also may be one in us.

—John 17:21

Oneness

I had a long chat with a pastor who is trained in counseling and has been very helpful to many. Often medical doctors refer patients to him. He says, "In every case of separation and divorce, the problem is oneness. Either the couple never achieved it or lost it."

What is oneness?

Oneness is planning together, playing together, working together.

Oneness is openness, honesty with each other.

Oneness is restraining selfish tendencies, directing personal preferences toward the family.

Oneness is forgiving and forgetting.

Oneness is thinking of the other's fears, hopes, dreams, feelings.

Oneness is physical fulfillment, but it is more. Those who say that physical oneness is the most important part of marriage are not right. It is big but not that big.

Oneness is worshiping, praying, talking about

God together. Spiritual oneness is as necessary as physical oneness. Oneness is really a matter of the spirit, of the heart. As the scripture above says, Jesus prayed for us that we may be one, as He and His Father are one. This prayer can find answer in you and me.

Can couples achieve oneness even if they never have had oneness or lost it? Yes, oh, yes, if they really want to. It is really worth the effort.

I will therefore that men pray every where, lifting up holy hands, without wrath and doubting.

—1 Tim. 2:8

Pray, Brother!

Does prayer really change things? Would God move things around because I prayed?

Call it what you may . . . coincidence, simple thinking, or what . . . I see answers to prayer. Surely it could be that I can't see all of the problem, nor understand even what I do see, but enough is seen for me to praise the Lord!

God is love, and love longs to lift, strengthen, touch, and care for the loved one. God is occupied not only with planets, suns, attractions and repulsions, world systems of weather, and laws of birth and death . . . God so loved the world (His friends, His people, His own, His rebelling creation) that He gave. It seems easy for me to see God break through the normal processes of healing to speed someone's recovery. I see it and shout.

Prayer is necessary, for we need God more than the thing we pray for. The real need is to know God, to feel God, to have God, to think His thoughts. "Communion with God is the one need of a man beyond all needs," said George McDonald. And he continues by saying, "So begins a communion, a talking with God, a coming-to-one with Him, which is the sole end of prayer, yea, of existence itself in its infinite phases."

So let's pray, brother.

✤◗●◖✤

The Lord will give strength unto his people; the Lord will bless his people with peace.

—Ps. 29:11

Playing Games

Living is fun. Laughter is healing. Just forgetting and playing is good for all of us.

Some of the best memories of life were times of fun and games. Childish? Perhaps, but true.

In good games, everyone is equal. Men and boys, boys and girls, black and white, weak and strong. It isn't a good game if some are very strong and others weak.

We get close together in games. We are ourselves. We show our real selves. We trust our partners in games. Falseness shows up as we play.

We need each other in games. We really do. Even super-stars need the team to win. In family games, good games, the fun is in doing it together.

Games give us rest. Our troubles are left behind,

we lose ourselves in simple play. We laugh, we plan, we struggle in fun, we sleep and get up and go.

Life is more than a game. Fun is more than winning. The big moment of the big game will pass. Even super-stars are forgotten. Rick Mount, a three-time all-American at Purdue University, was proud of the sign at the edge of his hometown. It said, "Home of Rick Mount." But he didn't become an instant success in the professional ranks. Now he is doing other things. He says in fun, "One night a windstorm blew down the sign, and no one bothered to put it back up."

So we can't play all the time. But stop now and then, play awhile, rest, then laugh and work again.

Remove far from me vanity and lies:
give me neither poverty nor riches;
feed me with food convenient for me.
—Prov. 30:8

Questions I Will Not Ask

To me it is funny when someone asks a question and then gets an answer he really didn't want to hear. Like this:

"Tell me, friend, why didn't I get elected? Confidentially—tell me."

So you tell him how overbearing he is. But he didn't really want to know, and you lost a friend. Here follow some questions I will not ask:

"Frankly, now—how old do you think I am?" Why tempt your friend to exaggerate?

"Will you stop me when I talk too much?" You just know he will.

"I've really never made it; can you tell me why?" You know why—don't you?

"If you were to do what I'm trying to do, how would you do it?" This might be a good question if you really mean it and if you can take constructive criticism.

"Why did you do that? You knew better, didn't

you?" I never ask this question. I'm not his judge nor even a private investigator.

"Why are you wearing that? In training for gymnastics?" He could look worse, and you may look worse.

"Are you Italian or Indian?" Why be curious? He's a brother in the family of God.

Any other questions?

He flattereth himself in his own eyes, until his iniquity be found to be hateful.

—Ps. 36:2

Rate Yourself!

(For father, husband, wife, mother. Score each characteristic 0 to 10, then forget it.)

1. I am available. If the children have a problem, I am there. Yet I urge them and encourage them to solve their own problems. _____

2. I have a sense of humor. I can even laugh at myself.

3. I am fair. I praise and reprove carefully.

4. I am patient. I remember (yes, I do) that I was young years ago. _____

5. I am able to make decisions. And I can change my mind when I should. _____

6. I am content with my lot in life . . . not envious of others. _____

7. I am prayerful . . . God is real to me.

8. I am committed in love to Jesus Christ

. . . my Saviour, my Friend, my Lord, my
King.   _____

TOTAL _____

Now how about asking someone to rate *you*?
(Ask your husband or wife or children, and don't
fret about the results.)

Unto him that is able to do exceeding abundantly above all that we ask or think, according to the power that worketh in us, unto him be glory.

—EPH. 3:20

Saints on Third Street

Most of us don't have great experiences: like eating with kings and queens, supping with the president or prime minister. We do well if we get within 70 feet of Billy Graham. Every day is much like every other day. Up and at it . . . same lunch from the same lunch box. And about all we do around the house is to do the dishes, mow the lawn, spank the children, pay some bills, and worry about others.

But do you know something? We can live common lives in an uncommon manner. We can keep a standard of conduct and conversation that glorifies our Lord. We can be honest and careful in our business affairs as if Jesus were our Auditor. We can with joy attend the church, pay our tithe, pray with our family, seek for ways to share Christ with our neighbors.

It is our privilege to "live common lives in an uncommon manner." Dr. J. B. Chapman said that, and he said this too: "To be patient when others would become irritable, to be cheerful when others are possessed with fear, to be kind when others are resentful, to be pure when others would break under temptation, to reject all price offered for doing wrong, to just show the spirit of the Master in common places among common people." This is real victory.

A man hath joy by the answer of his mouth: and a word spoken in due season, how good is it!"

—PROV. 15:23

Table Manners

"Now don't reach in front of your brother for your favorite piece of chicken. Just wait until it comes by. If you live long enough, your special piece will be at your place; wait at least one time!" (This theory of Mother's was hard to believe and harder to practice, but it saved a few fork wounds . . . and seeking for position causes wounds too!)

"When Dr. Goodwin comes, please be a little quieter, Paul." (It is wholesome to see people who sparkle when no one new or great is around.)

"Alright, he has a black eye. I don't want anyone looking at him, giggling, or even asking him how it happened. If he wants to tell us, fine; otherwise, forget it!" (I've hurt too many people with careless, caustic, playful attacks. And I've been hurt too, and deserved it.)

"Yes, you will wear your Sunday shirt!" (I'm just human enough to enjoy being with people who go to just a little effort to be with me; I am no better than they. A cleaned, ironed shirt is no better than a wrinkled one, but I felt better that they changed!)

"Dad, will you say grace." (It was a high moment for me. My son and daughter-in-law were entertaining guests in London. Musician friends, artists, and students were there, and the table was set with good food. We were seated. Gloria, my daughter-in-law, invited me to pray. Just a little gesture . . . just right.)

Good living with good friends is helped by good manners. What do you think?

⋘◉▮◉⋙

There is a way that seemeth right unto a man, but the end thereof are the ways of death.

—PROV. 16:25

Testimony of Dennis Hayes

Dennis Hayes, detective in the Homicide Division, Metropolitan Police, Washington, D.C., says, "It is a long story—a good story—of how I came to Christ. But briefly, it is the story of the surrender of self. A crisis in my life. Things at home were no better . . . as a matter of fact, they were worse. I was angry . . . I couldn't do what I wanted to do. I began to ponder leaving my wife, leaving my family. I know you are asking, How could I do that? Run from a good family, beautiful children, a good wife? It is easy when you are selfish. It is easy when you think you are the only thing in the world. I got busier on the job. I found it convenient to be gone as much as possible. At home, I was lazy; I gave no help with the children. I was cross and complaining."

He continued, "One day God talked to me while I was sitting in the middle of my own living room. He told me that I could not leave my family . . . not because they needed me, but because I needed them. Jesus showed me through His Word how selfish I was. I did nothing unless I received praise. I took all the successes to myself and put all the failures on my wife. He said, 'Give up your selfish life, your hateful self, your miserable self. I will give you life, real life . . . life that you didn't think was possible.' I took the deal! Praise God . . . it is true."

Touching the Almighty, we cannot find him out: he is excellent in power, and in judgment, and in plenty of justice: he will not afflict.

—Job 37:23

Unlucky?

Here's a funny, complicated rhyme:
> *The rain falls on the just and the unjust fellow.*
> *But more upon the just,*
> *For the unjust has the just's umbrella.*

Blaming is an easy way out, even when we just blame our bad luck. No one's "luck runs out," nor is anyone "plain unlucky."

This is our Father's world. It is orderly, reasonable. The suffering, starvation, war, misery is the work of the evil one in the hearts of men.

Acts of God seem tragic to some . . . things like storms and earthquakes . . . while to others they may have reason. Some storms are actually a blessing.

I suppose what I am trying to say is that we will all feel better and things will seem to fall in order better if we just praise the Lord. Make it more than just a vocabulary change. See the Lord in all things. See the "unlucky" thing as a challenge to turn it to

God's glory. An old-timer said, "Change luck to pluck and you'll win."

You know, when you really feel low, unlucky, or put down, read the Book of Job. It is up-to-date, God-centered, and beautiful. It is God speaking to us. "God thundereth marvellously with his voice; great things doeth he, which we cannot comprehend" (Job 37:5).

Poverty and shame shall be to him that refuseth instruction: but he that regardeth reproof shall be honoured.
——Prov. 13:18

Weather Vanes for Troubles

Red sky in the morning, sailors take warning;
Red sky at night, sailors' delight.

If we would just look for them, there are warnings of trouble in our homes and in our lives. If we saw them and made necessary adjustments and corrections, we would have peace.

I will try to list some simple signs that often warn of trouble. These are my ideas . . . could be exaggerated. But here they are:

1. Calling names. This leads to unpleasantness. It seems like fun at first, but this kind of fun gets old.

2. Yelling at each other. Check the noise level in your house.

3. Being too busy to enjoy each other. Love in our homes is more important than all the gadgets or dollars in the world.

4. Believing hearsay and rumors. This really does give trouble. I said it before, and here it is

again: "A real friend never believes rumors about you and even makes allowance for the facts."

5. Putting each other down. Making fun of good attempts . . . laughing at honest effort. Deep hurts begin right here.

6. Spending more than we earn. Then tithing becomes a chore . . . arguments arise . . . tension mounts.

7. Putting something before God. Just letting it happen . . . by default, by being too busy, by forgetting. Any way it happens, it is dangerous to keep God in second place.

Just some warnings I had on my mind. You probably know more and better ones, I'm sure. But let's keep them in mind and take care.

The Lord is my shepherd; I shall not want.

—Ps. 23:1

Wanted

You know what the kids want? And it doesn't take money . . . just love and time.

Here's the way the "Wanted" sign looks . . . in children's eyes.

WANTED: PEOPLE WHO CAN:

Hug . . . your strong arms are needed. There is so much to frighten.

Listen . . . most people talk too much. And listen like you would want to be listened to.

Play, swim, and hike . . . you might not be as good as we are.

Cry . . . not all the time . . . but once in a while it really helps.

Teach . . . there are a few things we do not know. Tell us. Show us.

Tickle . . . laughing does a lot for us.

Pray . . . God is real to us. Tell us about Him. Show us how to find Him.

Then were there brought unto him little children, that he should put his hands on them, and pray: and the disciples rebuked them.

—MATT. 19:13

Who Works Harder?

I borrowed this story from Rev. Morris Wilson, outstanding pastor in Rochester, N.Y.

A busy businessman argued with his wife about who worked the hardest, he as a bookkeeper on the job or his wife at home. So the good man offered to stay home one day in her place and keep a record of his activities. They would see whose job was hardest.

Here is his report: "On this day I did the following: Opened doors for children 106 times, closed the door for children 106 times . . . tied their shoes 16 times . . . rescued baby, who is learning to creep, 21 times . . . told two-year-old Georgie 'Don't' 94 times, and Georgie yelled, 'Don't,' 2 times . . . stopped quarrels 16 times . . . spread peanut butter and jelly on bread 11 times (and a few times on the kids) . . . issued cookies 30 times . . . served drinks 15 times . . . answered the telephone 7 times . . . wiped noses 19 times . . . answered questions 145 times, stumped by questions 175 times . . . lost my temper 45 times, and ran after the children 4½ miles."

So, let's be happy in our work . . . give others credit for their work . . . and thank God for the privilege of working even with children. They are important. Even you were a child once.

Lest there be any fornicator or profane person, as Esau, who for one morsel of meat sold his birthright.

—Heb. 12:16

X-rated

Common things tend to be cheap. Marriage is common . . . tends to be cheapened. Sex is common . . . and some make it cheap.

But life is precious. Sex is beautiful too. It is a good side of marriage. My friend Charles Higgins says: "Sex is not a favor to give or withhold. It should not be a weapon to dominate nor a reward for good actions. Sex should not be just a selfish, personal pleasure." It is giving and receiving love, sharing and caring. It is a beautiful dimension of love.

This might be just the place to add these things: We are not just animals. Your partner is made in the image of God. She or he will live forever. We were created, we are sustained, we are precious in the plan of God. Our bodies, our hunger, our needs are sacred. Then discipline, carefulness in caring for them is important. Esau, says God's Word, was a fornicator, one who played with precious things. He traded his birthright for a bowl of stew! Foolish, of course, but there are Esaus around today, playing disrespectfully with beautiful things.

I can . . . you can . . . do our little bit, by example, by careful counsel, to keep precious these common experiences.

*Thou feedest them with the bread of
tears; and givest them tears to drink in
great measure.*

—Ps. 80:5

Your Tears

Were you embarrassed when you were caught
wiping your eyes?

Did it do you in when tears came, uncalled and
unwanted?

I found this item in the *Los Angeles Times:* "After the salad luncheon came the film on the Guide
Dogs Training School in San Rafael. At the end of
the very moving documentary, Mrs. Ogden Vest,
Mrs. Paul Selwyn, Mrs. Michael Fosman, Mrs.
Armand Oppenheim, and Charlotte Kalik were just
a few caught wiping their eyes." How about that.
No description of their clothes or jewelry. Their
names listed because they cried. But the article went
on, "Norah Hamilton reassured them by saying, 'If
you don't cry after that film, you don't belong
here.'" And that's all right too.

If you can't cry a little, don't plan on being in
love. When you care enough, there'll be times when
you can't keep the tears back.

If you can't cry a little, don't plan on being a parent. You might not be able to hide your tears all the time either. Maybe you shouldn't try.

If you can't cry a little, your misery will grow and grow.

It just might be a better world, a better home where we are, if more of us were caught in the act of wiping tears . . . even if we didn't get our name in the paper.

$\textbf{Z}$

Jacob awaked out of his sleep, and he said, Surely the Lord is in this place; and I knew it not.

—GEN. 28:16

Z-z-z—The Good Sound of Sleep

"Please go away and let me sleep. Sleep to me is a real treat. I'd rather sleep than eat. So please go away, so I can sleep."

Sleeping is a treat. Some are missing this treat. Are you? Long nights, haunting memories, nagging problems, a host of fears—these fill the room night after night. We need rest but we do not get it. We worry about our restlessness, and this keeps us from resting. Around and around . . . nights of misery. We really hate to see the sun go down!

Some things seem to do little for us—things like pills, for instance. They have their place, I'm sure, but addiction is worse than sleeplessness. All forms of "running away," whether pills, drugs, alcohol, or feverish activity seem to just delay the real solution.

Have you tried these things recently?

1. *Praying.* Yes, simple, trusting, childlike prayer. Tell Him, trust Him. Wrap all your burdens